Candlecraft

Candlecraft

Paul Marko and Debbie Davis

Oceana

An Oceana Book

This book is published by
Oceana Books
The Old Brewery.
6 Blundell Street
London N 7 9BH

ISBN 1-86160-213-8
OCEXAW

Project Manager: Rebecca Kingsley
Project Editor: Sarah Harris
Designer: Bruce Low
Photography: Ian Hessenberg

Typeset in Sabon
Manufactured in Singapore by Eray Scan Pte Ltd
Printed in Singapore by Star Standard Industries Pte. Ltd.

CONTENTS

INTRODUCTION – **6**

CHAPTER 1 – SAFETY – **10**

CHAPTER 2 – EQUIPMENT AND MATERIALS – **13**

CHAPTER 3 – HOW TO USE THIS BOOK – **16**

CHAPTER 4 – MAKING CANDLES WITH MOULDS – **17**

CHAPTER 5 – DIPPED CANDLES AND OVERDIPPING – **49**

CHAPTER 6 – SPECIAL EFFECTS AND TECHNIQUES – **65**

CHAPTER 7 – WORKING WITH BEESWAX – **105**

CHAPTER 8 – ADVANCED PROCEDURES – **113**

CHAPTER 9 – PROBLEMS AND HOW TO SOLVE THEM – **118**

GLOSSARY – **124**

INDEX – **126**

Introduction

Looking at the variety of candles available today – from sophisticated dining room tapers to multi-coloured candles of all shapes and sizes, it is hard to imagine that candles are believed to have first been used by the Ancient Egyptians, around 3000 years BC. At that time, however, they bore little resemblance to the candles we are familiar with. These early candles were more like flaming torches, made of reed and tallow - a substance similar to suet.

Although the Romans did use tallow torches, they are also given credit for developing the first wick candles. Primarily these were found in temples and other places of worship, but richer households were also able to obtain them for domestic usage. The word candle itself actually derives from the Latin, 'candere', meaning to flicker or glitter. And flicker they most certainly did! Tallow was smoky and acrid, and burned poorly, so when the first beeswax candles were introduced during the Middle Ages, it was a major advance. Beeswax candles burn steadily, and do not give off unpleasant aromas. Unfortunately, during their early years, they were very labour-intensive to produce, making them too expensive for any but the richest people to afford.

Candles in some shape or form were in use throughout most parts of the world during the Middle Ages, although some were more effective than others. The Japanese were using the rather unpleasant method of obtaining wax from boiling insects. Olive

oil formed the main ingredient for candles in Mediterranean countries, while in America candle wax came from boiled berries. The candles made in these ways had two basic flaws. Firstly the flame they provided was erratic, causing them to burn poorly, and they were also generally uneconomical to produce.

It took until the nineteenth century for major steps to be taken in the development of candle making. In 1825, a Frenchman called Cambaceres produced a braided wick that finally solved the problem of erratic burning. With one thread tighter than the others, a braided wick gradually trims itself to the correct length as it burns.

Prior to this, candles had a single wick which often burned unevenly, making it necessary for them to be snuffed regularly – sometimes as often as every thirty minutes.

Although this new form of wick meant that candles produced were now far more efficient, candle makers were still limited in the number of candles they could create. Each candle had to be made by hand - a time-consuming process. Yet, as with so many traditional crafts in the nineteenth century, candle making was transformed by the Industrial Revolution. In 1834, Joseph Morgan invented a machine that could produce moulded candles at a rate of

around 1500 per hour. This mass production of candles meant that for the first time they began to become a common household commodity.

Perhaps the greatest development, however, was the introduction of paraffin wax – a by-product of crude petroleum – as an alternative to beeswax. Like beeswax, the blue-tinged white paraffin-wax burns cleanly and without producing any unpleasant aroma. However, paraffin-wax has one major advantage over beeswax – it is considerably cheaper to produce and buy. Inevitably, with the coming of electricity, the requirement for candles as a household necessity began to diminish. Although more remote regions may still rely on candles as their primary source of light, those in the developed world generally view candles as attractive accessories, used mainly for ornament or as relaxation aids. Having said that, there can be few households even in today's electricity-dependent societies without a few candles tucked away in case of power cuts!

With candles playing such an important role in life throughout history, it is little wonder that there are numerous references

to them in literature. Shakespeare often utilised candle metaphors, and one particularly famous example appears in Macbeth, where the burning down of the candle represents the brief passage of time,

..out, out, brief candle!
Life's but a walking shadow, a poor player,
that struts and frets his hour upon the stage,
And then is heard no more...

He also speaks of candles lighting the shadows of life in The Merchant of Venice;

Portia: How far that little candle throws his beams,
So shines a good deed in a naughty world.

Developments in the mass-production of candles mean that candles in all shapes, colours and sizes are readily available, from elegant dining room tapers to scented, mood-enhancing candles. It would be easy to imagine, therefore, that the craft of the hand-made candle would have been lost, but this is far from the case. Designers still create beautiful and original hand-crafted candles, and more and more people are choosing candle-making as a hobby.

Whether mass-produced or created at home, the basic concept of candle-making is the same as it has been for centuries. With the help of this book and its projects, you will be able to understand this concept and produce your own candles from the most basic of materials and using a variety

of equipment, much of which can be found either outdoors, or in your own home.

CHAPTER ONE

Safety

■ ■ ■

Making candles is similar to cookery in many ways, and, as with cooking, there is a potential element of messiness, and the possibility of unforeseen accidents, both large and small. To cut down on these, and to be ready for any eventuality, please read the following carefully.

● Always wear old clothes, cover work surfaces with newspaper and move or cover rugs and carpets.

● Keep a pile of old newspapers close to hand in case of spillage.

● Always give yourself plenty of room to work in and keep your work space clean and tidy.

● Have all the materials and equipment to hand for whichever project you are working on.

● Keep all equipment clean and keep unused materials in containers away from dust and dirt.

Take care when pouring hot wax to avoid spillages

Using Wax

When using wax, treat it as you would cooking oil. Below 100°C (212°F) it is fairly safe. Higher than this it is likely to catch fire as the wax is turning to vapour.

Always place your thermometer in the saucepan at the beginning of the melting process. This will not only ensure your temperature reading is accurate, but will also prevent you inadvertently overheating the wax.

Never leave heating wax unattended.

If wax is overheating, it begins to smoke and gives off an acrid smell. If this happens, turn off the heat source immediately and allow the wax to cool.

Wax can be removed easily from metal

Should the worst happen:
● Switch off the heat
● Do not move the pan
● Smother flames with either the saucepan lid or a damp cloth/blanket
● On no account attempt to douse with water – this will only spread the fire

After use do not be tempted to pour excess molten wax down the sink as it will set and block your pipes. Instead pour it into an old baking tray and cut into cubes before it hardens. This can then be used to make chunk candles at a later date.
Alternatively, pour the excess wax into an old milk carton. The waxed interior will ease removal at a later date.

In case of spillage

For wax on carpets and items of clothing: Scrape off the excess wax and remove the rest by placing a paper towel over the stained area, and pressing with a hot iron. This will transfer the wax to the towel.

For wax on metal or plastic objects:
Place in the freezer for an hour to make the wax brittle. It then becomes easy to simply crumble the hardened wax away. Alternatively, dip the object into hot water and allow the wax to melt and float to the surface.

For smaller spillages, use a sparing amount of white spirit or turpentine to dissolve small areas of cold, dried wax. Then dab off with an old cloth or paper towels.

CANDLE TIPS

Never leave a burning candle unattended

Place candles in a secure area on a non-flammable holder

If you place a dark candle in a brass holder, watch that the colour does not bleed onto the surface

Place candles away from direct sunlight to avoid the dye fading

Marks or dust on a candle can be removed by polishing with a pair of nylon tights. These can also be used to regain the candle's original sheen, which tends to dull from the heat of the flame

Candles placed in the fridge will burn longer, but you must protect them from moisture. Never place candles in the freezer as they may crack

Burn candles in an area free from draughts. Even a dripless candle can drip if it is in a draught as the movement of air will make it burn unevenly. If this does happen, push the wick towards the highest point on the candle. The dripping may extinguish the candle at first, but the burning should eventually even out

To snuff out a candle and eliminate smoking, try dipping the wick into the melted wax with the end of a knife

To stop melted wax from splattering when blowing out a candle, simply cup your hand round the flame before you blow

Do not touch or trim the wick of a cold candle, as it is very fragile. If you break the small carbon cap of the wick you will have great difficulty when it comes to re-lighting.

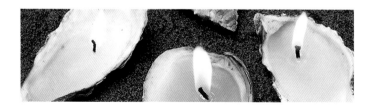

CHAPTER TWO

Equipment
and Materials

Before you start making the candles in the following projects you will need some basic equipment and tools. These are generally inexpensive and readily available from craft shops or by mail order. If you do not wish to spend too much initially, you will probably find that you already have many of the basic tools, or at least, adequate alternatives.

■ ■ ■

Left/right from top: scales, scissors, scalpel, thermometer, measuring cup.

HEAT SOURCE

For melting the paraffin wax, a domestic electric or gas cooker is ideal. Alternatively you can use a double burner picnic stove. This has the advantage of being portable so you can set up your workshop wherever you wish.

THERMOMETER

To measure the heat of your melting wax, a specialist wax thermometer covering the scale 38–177°C (100–350°F) is recommended.

DOUBLE BOILER

A double saucepan made from stainless steel or aluminium which is used for

WICKING NEEDLES

Used for inserting the wicks into your moulds. They can also be used for tying the wick at the base of moulds before the wax is poured. These are generally made of steel and measure between 10–25cm (4 – 10″) long.

DIPPING CAN

A tall cylindrical vessel used for holding hot wax. It must be deep and wide enough to allow the complete immersion of a candle. Professional dipping cans are made of metal and can be bought from craft shops. However, an asparagus boiler with the basket removed makes a suitable alternative. These can be bought from most kitchen shops.

Dipping Can

melting wax over boiling water. A double boiler is recommended, although one saucepan inside another can be used. Boil water in one, and melt your wax in the second. Do not leave the saucepans untended, as there is a risk that they may tip, spilling hot wax and water. Always hold the handles firmly. Purpose-made boilers can be obtained from craft or kitchen shops.

SCALES

Required to measure the amount of wax and other materials that you are using. Kitchen scales are ideal.

Plastic, metal and rubber moulds; wicking needle; wick and wick holder.

Above: Beeswax can be obtained in disk or sheet form, while paraffin wax comes in chunks or beads

MEASURING JUG

To determine how much wax you will need to fill your mould, first fill the mould with water, then pour the water into the jug. For every quarter pint of water you should use approximately 100g (4oz) of solid wax.

Below: A saucepan can be used in place of the double boiler when you begin.

OTHER USEFUL ITEMS

Washing up bowls for cooling candles

Old newspaper or paper towels for mopping up

Scalpel for trimming wax

Sharp scissors for cutting wicks

Old rounded spoon for smoothing wax

Old wooden spoon or knife for stirring dye into melted wax

Small weight to stop full moulds floating in a water bath

Old milk cartons for storing excess wax

Greaseproof paper

Tin foil

Old foil cake tins

Small measuring scoops

Releasing agent, such as silicone spray

CHAPTER THREE

How *to use* this Book

■ ■ ■

Our aim in this book is to introduce you to all areas of candle-making through a variety of different projects. The difficulty of the projects increases through the chapters, ranging from simple single-colour candles to elaborate designs and effects. Some you will find easy, while others may take patience, and several attempts, to perfect. Once you are happy that you have mastered the basic principles of each project, you may wish to experiment with your own ideas. All the projects are presented with clear, step-by-step instructions, and illustrated with easy to follow photographs and often extra tips and advice. With each project, we also show you either an idea for displaying your candles to their best advantage, or illustrate some more advanced candles you can create using the techniques described.

A chapter at the end of this book describes some of the most common faults you may find or make during the course of your work. In each case we show you how best to remedy any problems you may have.

Most of the projects here use basic and inexpensive tools and materials. However, in chapter 8 we show you some of the more specialised equipment you may wish to buy if you want to develop the craft of candle making a little further.

We hope that you will have fun with the projects in this book, and do remember that improvisation is an important part of any craft, so don't be afraid to experiment with colours, styles and techniques.

All projects feature clear step-by-step instructions

CHAPTER FOUR

Making Candles *with* Moulds

■ ■ ■

INTRODUCTION

Nowadays it is difficult to imagine what it must have been like making candles from tallow, but this excerpt taken from an Australian cookbook published as recently as 1956 will give you some idea:

"To 15 lb. of Mutton tallow (fat) add 1.25 lb. beeswax. Cut up wax and place fat in water. Boil 1 hour in large saucepan. Allow it to get cold then cut out the cake of fat and scrape off the soft under part. Cut up your fat and put into this, and add to it 5lb of alum and saltpetre. Skim carefully while it is simmering. When cold, take it out of the water. It is now ready to be rendered down and poured into the candle moulds."

Today the most basic ingredients you need to make a candle are wax and wick, both of which are readily available from candle making suppliers and craft shops. Before proceeding with this section, you will need to obtain the materials shown below. In all our projects we will tell you the approximate weight of wax, the size of wick and other quantities you will need.

Paraffin wax is available in either slab or bead form and is a by-product of the oil-refining industry. To begin with, we recommend that you use beads, rather than slabs, as beads are much easier to work with. As you progress you can move on to paraffin-wax slabs if you wish to try different methods. These beads are solid at room temperature, and melt to a colourless, odourless liquid at temperatures between 40°C and 71°C (105–160°F). For our projects, any paraffin wax in the melting range of 57–60°C (135–140°F) is suitable.

Wick comes in all types and sizes. The most suitable candle-making wicks are those of braided cotton, treated chemically to improve the quality of burning. Wick is sold in 1cm ($^1/_2$ inch) gradations and the size of your candle determines the size of your wick. For example if your finished candle is going to be 2.5cm (1 inch) in diameter, then use a 2.5cm (1 inch) wick. If your candle is 5cm (2 inches) in diameter then use a 5cm (2 inches) wick and so on.

Dye discs are used by candle makers to achieve a vast range of colours and shades. How much you use depends on the makeup of your wax and the size of the candle, but as a general rule 450g (1lb) of wax will require a quarter of a disc; 900g (2lb) will require half a disc and 2kg (4lb 6oz) will require 1 full disc.

Stearin is a useful additive to wax that increases the depth of the colour dyes, stops dripping and improves burning. It also increases the tendency of paraffin wax to shrink, which makes removing candles from rigid moulds much easier. Use 10% of stearin to weight of wax.

Do not use stearin in rubber moulds as it will rot them.

Vybar is an additive to wax that increases its opacity and helps it to burn better. Vybar reduces the shrinkage of paraffin wax, so is ideal when using rubber moulds. Allow 2.5g (0.1 oz) of vybar to 500g (20 oz) of wax.

Do not use vybar in rigid moulds as your candles will be difficult to remove.

Mould seal is similar to putty and is used to hold the wick in place. At the same time it prevents both wax leaking from the mould, and water seeping in. Mould seal is re-usable.

Most candles are made from moulds, and these come in all shapes and sizes. Materials used include plastic, metal, rubber, latex and glass. We will be using the first three in our projects.

RIGID PLASTIC MOULDS

Available in a variety of geometric shapes from hexagons and spheres to pyramids. You can also buy trays of repeated shapes which are ideal for floating candles. Care must be taken with these, as they are prone to warping and scratching.

METAL MOULDS

These have the advantage of being tough and sturdy, but the shapes available are limited, and they can be rather expensive.

RUBBER/LATEX MOULDS

The flexible material makes these extremely versatile. Not only can you achieve a large amount of detail and relief, but their flexibility enables you to make candles from odd shapes that could not be removed from a rigid mould. The main drawback to using rubber or latex moulds is that they have a limited life span.

Scented Oil

Pigment

Measuring Spoons

Gilding Wax

Dye Disks

Paraffin Beads

GLASS MOULDS

These give a high gloss finish to candles. As with metal moulds however, there are limited shapes available and they are very easy to break. A release agent must be used.

All of these moulds are readily available in commercial form. Later in this book we will be showing you how to improvise with various household items, and how to make your own latex moulds.

For projects in the following sections, the approximate weight of wax needed will be as follows:

For a 12.5cm (5″) high cone use 135g (5.5 oz) of wax

For an 11cm (4.5″) high cylinder use 250g (10 oz) of wax

For a 16cm (6.5″) high hexagon use 325g (13 oz) of wax

Using paraffin beads, stearin and dye discs.

A variety of moulds

Priming *your* Wick

This is a very quick and simple process which allows your finished candle to burn evenly. Every candle you make must have a primed wick. Make primed wicks in batches, rather than having to make one especially for each new project.

■　■　■

YOU WILL NEED

Double boiler

Thermometer

Tin foil or greaseproof paper

Wax pellets

A length (about an inch/2.5cm longer than a beeswax sheet) of 1″ wick

Step 1

Heat a small amount of wax pellets in the double boiler. When the temperature reaches about 70°C (158°F), turn off the heat.

Step 2

Take your length of wick and dip into the melted wax. Leave for a few seconds.

Step 3

Remove the wick when you see air bubbles at the surface. This means the wick has absorbed sufficient wax.

Step 4

Lay the wick in a straight line across the foil or greaseproof paper. After a few minutes the wick will become hard and ready to use.

Single Colour Cone

The simplest candles to make are those created using only one colour. The method used to make a single colour cone will form the basis of the projects to follow, so this simple, yet attractive, candle is an excellent starting point.

■   ■   ■

YOU WILL NEED

Double boiler
Thermometer
Wicking needle
Plastic cone mould
Bowl of water
Scissors
Kitchen scales
Weight
Wax beads
Stearin
Dye disc (any colour)
Primed 1″ wick
(as project 1)
Mould seal

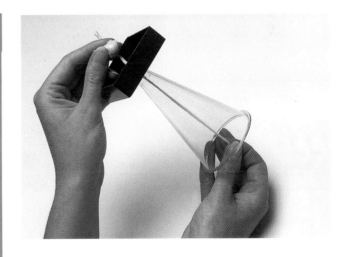

Step 1

Wicking up the mould.

Put one end of the primed wick through the hole at the base of the mould. Let it protrude about 2.5cm and seal the hole well with mould seal.

Step 2

Lay the wicking needle across the base of the mould. Gently pull the wick taut and tie around the wicking needle. IMPORTANT: always place the wick through the centre of your candle unless otherwise stated.

Step 3

Melt the stearin in the double boiler, then add the dye and dissolve. To colour about 200g (8 oz) of paraffin wax you will need approximately 2.5g (0.1 oz) of a dye disc. Add the paraffin wax and heat to 90°C (194°F).

Step 4

Carefully pour the wax into the mould. Wait one minute, then sharply tap the sides of the mould to bring any air bubbles to the surface. Place the mould in the bowl of water and weight it down. Leave to cool.

Step 5

After about one hour a well will start to appear around the wick which will need to be topped up with liquid wax. Remove the mould from the water and gently pierce the surface around the well with a sharp tool - scissors, a scalpel or your wicking needle are ideal.

Step 6

Re-heat the wax to 93°C (199°F) and top up the mould. Be careful not to exceed the original level of the wax. Allow to cool for a few hours.

Step 7

When cool, remove the mould seal. Cut off the wicking needle, tip up the mould and your candle should slide out. Trim your wick to 1/4" (6cm) and level off the base. You can do this by placing the candle base down in a warm saucepan or use a scalpel to trim a level base.

Multi-Coloured Candle

Brightly coloured objects always have visual appeal, and candles are no exception. In this project, different colours are layered to produce a striking effect. Once you are confident with the technique, why not try experimenting with different colour combinations – whether clashing or complementary – to suit your own colour schemes.

■   ■   ■

YOU WILL NEED

Double boiler
Thermometer
Scissors
Wicking needle
Mould seal
Cylindrical mould
Bowl of water
Weight
Wax beads
Blue dye disc
Pink dye disc
Black dye disc
Primed 1″ wick,
25g (1 oz) stearin

Step 1

Wick up and seal your cylindrical mould. Divide your wax beads and stearin into 3 even batches.

27

Step 2

Heat one batch of stearin in the double boiler and add enough of the black dye disc to colour one portion of the wax. Dissolve. Add one batch of wax beads and heat to 90°C (194°F). Gently pour into the cylindrical mould, being careful not to let the wax touch the sides of the mould. Let the wax cool until the surface is rubbery and warm to the touch.

Step 3

Heat the second batch of stearin, this time adding the blue dye disc. Dissolve. Add the second batch of wax pellets and heat to 90°C (194°F). Gently pour into the cylindrical mould and again leave to cool. Repeat step with the pink dye disk. Place and weight down in the water bath.

Step 4

As this final batch of wax cools, remove from the bath, pierce around the well and top up with melted wax.

Step 5

When the candle is cool enough, cut your wick from the wicking needle. Tip up your mould and let your finished candle slide out.

Angled Multi-Coloured Candle

By placing your mould at different angles, you can create interesting variations on the multi-coloured candle produced in Project 3. Experiment with different mould positions to find the shape you prefer. For this project we have chosen to use two colours for dramatic effect. As we have used a cone rather than a cylinder mould, less wax is needed.

■   ■   ■

YOU WILL NEED

Double boiler
Thermometer
Scissors
Wicking needle
Mould seal
Cone mould
Bowl of water
Cloth or old sponge for support
Weight
Wax beads
Primed 1″ wick
Stearin
Different colour dye disks

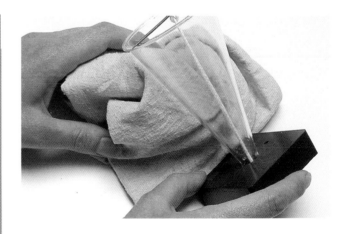

Step 1

Wick up the cone mould with a 1″ wick, leaning it at an angle against a balled up piece of cloth or sponge to support it. Weigh out your wax and stearin.

Step 2

Pour the first batch of colour into your mould and allow to cool – as in project 2. Then add second batch of wax, and allow to cool.

Step 3

For the last batch of wax you will need to tip the mould into the upright position before pouring.

Step 4

Top up the wax, and cut the wick from the needle as in previous projects. When cool, tip up and slide candle out.

Chunk Candle

Now you can use the excess pieces of wax left over from previous projects to create a pretty, multi-coloured candle. You can use any amount of colour chunks according to the effect you hope to achieve. For best results the chunks should be 12 – 25cm (¹/2 – 1in) in size. Sometimes you will not have enough scrap wax, so the first steps in this project will show you how to make your own chunks. We have used a star mould for this project, but any other shape will be just as attractive.

YOU WILL NEED

Double boiler
Thermometer
Mould
Scissors
Wicking needle
Old baking tray
Aluminium foil or foil pie tray
(make sure there are no holes
for wax to leak through)
Bowl of water
Weight
Wax beads
Stearin
Leftover coloured wax from
previous projects
Dye discs
1″ wick
Mould seal

Step 1

In your double boiler, heat up some stearin and enough dye disc to make a strong colour. Add enough wax pellets to cover your foil dish to a depth of about 1.5cm (¹/2″). Heat to 82°C (180°F) and pour into the foil dish or baking tray. Leave to cool.

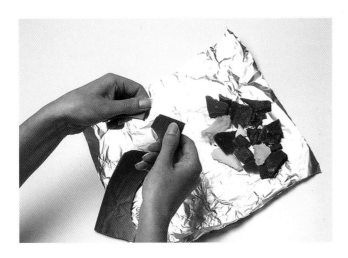

Step 2

When cooled, break the wax into small pieces You now have your chunks.

Step 3

Wick up and seal your mould, making sure that the wick goes through the centre. Put your chunks into the mould.

Step 4

Heat stearin and wax pellets to 93°C (199°F) and pour into your mould. Place into the water bath and weight down until cooled.

Step 5

Then remove from bath and top up wax as required. Remove candle from mould as before.

Chunk *and* Dye Candles

A variation on the previous project which produces a very brightly coloured candle. Again you can experiment with as few or as many colours as you like. We find that combining two different colours will get the best effect and that is we will be doing in this project.

■ ■ ■

YOU WILL NEED

Double boiler
Thermometer
Small saucepan
Tin cans. (These must be clean
and dry. Before you start, place
them into the saucepan, which
must be small enough so that
they cannot tip sideways when
placed in the water).
Wicking needle

2 spoons
Mould
Scissors
Bowl of water
Weight
Wax beads
Stearin
2 dye discs
Prepared chunks of
coloured wax

Step 1
Wick up the mould and place your chunks inside as before.

Step 2
Bring to boil about 5cm (2″) of water in the small saucepan, then turn down the heat to a very gentle simmer. Put chunks of dye disc and stearin into the cans and place into saucepan. The cans must not touch the bottom of the pan but must float about 1.5cm (½″) from the bottom. Add more or less water if necessary. If the cans tip up, place an empty can into the saucepan for balance. Heat until melted, then remove pan from heat.

Step 3
Heat the wax pellets and stearin in the double boiler to 93°C (199°F) and pour into the mould. Then take some dye from one of the cans with a spoon, and pour this into one side of the mould. Using the other spoon, pour colour from the second can into the other side of the mould.

Step 4
Leave for a minute, then place into water bath and weight down. When cool, remove mould and top up with wax. Remove wicking needle and mould seal

Bead Candles

The shape and size of paraffin wax beads makes them ideally suited for creating this most unusual and attractive of candles. Once you have mastered the technique, try experimenting with different colours, or quantities of beads.

■ ■ ■

YOU WILL NEED

Double boiler
Thermometer
Wicking needle
Scissors
Cylindrical mould
Wax beads
Dye disc
Stearin
Mould seal
1"wick

Step 1
Wick up your mould, and fill loosely with a number of wax pellets.

Step 2

Heat the stearin and dye until dissolved, then add wax pellets and heat to 93°C (199°F).

Step 3

Pour mixture into the mould. Top up when cooled, then cut off wicking needle.

Step 4

Remove mould seal, and slide out your candle as before. You will see the beaded effect immediately.

Scented Candle

While a lighted candle can give ambience, a scented one can help suggest a mood. Cinnamon and cloves give a festive scent for Christmas, Frankincense and Patchouli create an Eastern mood, while Jasmine produces a fresh, spring-like fragrance. For more practical purposes, lemongrass can be used to eliminate old tobacco smells.

■ ■ ■

Candles can also be used for aromatherapy. Burning a candle with the essential oils of lavender and sandalwood, for example, can induce a feeling of calmness. Not all scented oils are suitable for candle making, however. In some, the alcohol, and therefore the scent, will evaporate, and others will simply not mix. Though it is worth buying oils specifically made for the purpose from craft shops, there is nothing wrong with using what you find about the house for the purposes of experimentation.

Warning: certain oils can speed up the rot of rubber moulds and can cloud the surface of rigid plastic moulds.

YOU WILL NEED

Double boiler

Thermometer

Wooden spoon

Wicking needle

Square mould

Wax beads

Stearin

Dye disc

Scented candle oil

2" wick

Step 1

Wick up your mould and seal as before. Dissolve stearin and dye. Add wax pellets and heat to 82°C (180°F). Remove from heat.

Step 2

Add the scented oil. If using candle-making oil, follow the instructions carefully. Otherwise about ten drops will suffice. Stir.

Step 3

Pour mixture into mould. Leave for one minute. Tap, then place and weight down in the waterbath. Top up and de-mould as before.

Variations

Make a dark red candle and add 2 teaspoons of powdered cinnamon and cloves. This can be done in two ways. Either add before pouring, or after the candle is made. Try lighting the candle and letting it burn for half an hour, then adding the mixture to the melted pool of wax. The scent is delicious. For an extra festive touch, decorate with scrim or ribbon, or tie on cinnamon sticks.

Floating
Candles

A bowl of floating candles can bring ambience to any room. They look beautiful displayed in a bowl decorated with glass beads, although almost any container can be used – both in and out of doors. Try adding scent to your initial mix for aromatic floating candles. These candles can be made in special moulds or you may wish to shape them by hand.

■   ■   ■

YOU WILL NEED

Double boiler

Pastry cutters

Baking tray

Foil

Scissors

Wicking needle

¹/₂″ wick

Wax beads

Stearin

Dye disc

Step 1
Prime wick and cut into 2.5cm (1″) lengths. Line baking tray with foil.

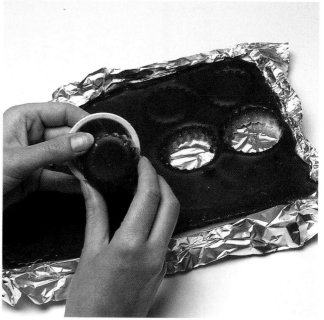

Step 2

Dissolve stearin and dye. Add wax pellets. Heat to 82°C (180°F). Pour into the baking tray to a depth of approximately 2cm (³/₄"). Leave to cool until malleable.

Step 3

Place the pastry cutter over the wax and gently push down. Lift up and gently push out the wax.

Step 4

Thread the wick through the middle by gently pushing into the wax, or make a hole with the wicking needle first.

Try experimenting with different colours and shapes. To mould your floating candles by hand, simply cut chunks of the cooled wax while it is rubbery and malleable, and shape as you wish.

Church Candles

Church candles, traditionally cream or off-white, look and smell beautiful and are easy to make. Metal moulds are best for these candles, but they do get very hot, so avoid touching them until they have cooled. Church candles contain beeswax which increases the burning time. However, beeswax tends to make the candle stick to the mould, so to aid release you will need to use a special agent.

■ ■ ■

YOU WILL NEED

Metal pillar mould

Thermometer

Wicking needle

Bowl of water

Double boiler

Mould seal

Wax beads

Stearin

Beeswax beads (approx. 10-25% of weight of wax beads)

Releasing agent (silicon spray)

Step 1

Treat the inside of the mould with release agent.

Step 3

Heat the stearin and wax pellets to 90°C (194°F), remove from heat and add the beeswax. Stir until dissolved.

Step 2

Let dry and then wick up. You will need to pay extra attention to the sealing, as the heat in metal moulds sometimes melts the mould seal.

Step 5

Holding the mould securely in place, fill the bowl with water. Then fill the mould with the remaining wax. Tap out any air bubbles and leave to cool.

Step 4

Fill a quarter of the mould with this wax mix. This will help weigh down the mould, and keep it in position when you place it in the bowl.

Step 6

Top up candle base, then remove from mould as before. You may wish to decorate with scrim, or leave plain.

Fruit Candle

Making a realistic candle fruit is fun and easy to do. We have chosen an orange to start with, as it is a simple shape - although once you are proficient you can produce a whole basket of different fruits if you wish. Making these candles is now easier than ever, thanks to the availability of combined dye and scent discs — so your orange will not only look realistic, it will smell good too.

■   ■   ■

YOU WILL NEED

Rubber orange mould
Double boiler
Thermometer
Bowl of water
Cardboard (big enough to fit over the bowl of water)
Washing up liquid
Wax beads
Orange dye/perfume disc
Vybar
I ¹/₂″ wick

Step I

You will need to make a support collar that will rest on the bowl of water and balance the rubber mould. Take a fairly stiff piece of cardboard and cut a circle in the middle big enough to hold your mould. Make a cut from the circle to the outside edge to aid mould removal later on.

Step 2

Using the wicking needle, draw your wick through the mould, taking care not to pierce the rubber in any other place. Fit the mould into the support cardboard.

Step 3

Melt the wax in the double boiler. Add the dye/perfume disc and vybar. Heat to 90°C (194°F) and pour into the mould. Tap out air bubbles and place the support over the water bath with the mould immersed in the water.

Step 4

Keep breaking the surface as the wax cools to top up if necessary. When cold, peel off the mould. To ease removal, coat the outside of the mould with a mixture of washing up liquid and water.

CHAPTER FIVE

Dipped Candles *and* Overdipping

■ ■ ■

INTRODUCTION

In our previous projects we have been focusing on relatively simple candles. As you have been progressing through them you will have become more confident and experienced, so now we will move on projects that will extend your techniques and introduce you to more unusual candlemaking methods and materials.

In this section we will be experimenting with overdipping, a process that has remained unchanged for centuries, and which can be used to produce anything from an elegant taper to a peeled fruit candle. Overdipping is a technique whereby a coloured candle is coated with a layer of contrasting colour wax or waxes.

To successfully work through this section, you will need to use a variety of different materials. We will briefly look at each of these before beginning the projects.

The first thing to understand is the difference between pigment and dye.

Pigment is used in overdipping wax and dye is used in candle wax. Pigment is stronger than dye and the colour is more intensive and doesn't fade.

Overdipping wax is a combination of resins and waxes that gives candles a tough and shiny coating.

Beautiful tapers can be produced by dipping

Dipped Dinner Tapers

Dipping candles is one of the simplest and oldest methods of making candles, whether done by hand or by machine. Commercial candles can be created from powdered wax which is then overdipped on a production line. Although candles produced this way are attractive, home-made candles have a special quality of their own. The most popular type of dipped candle is the elegant dinner candle, usually called a taper because of the shape it takes as it is dipped.

YOU WILL NEED

Dipping can
Very large saucepan
Thin piece of wood with 2 small hooks about 4cm (1.5") apart. This wood needs to be long enough to bridge the dipping can
Thermometer
Wooden spoon
Wax beads
Stearin
Dye disc
1" wick

3kg (7.5lb) of paraffin wax and 3 dye discs will make approximately six 25cm (10") dinner candles.

Step 1

Put the dipping can in a saucepan half full of water. Put stearin and dye into the dipping can and heat up gently until the mix liquefies. Fill the can $^3/_4$ full of wax beads. The can needs to be $^3/_4$ full of liquid wax so add extra beads as the wax melts until you reach the desired quantity. Heat to 71°C (160°F), then turn down the heat.

Step 2

Prime your wick and place it over the two hooks so that both ends hang down to a distance of 2.5cm (1″) from the bottom of the can.

Step 3

Dip the wicks into the dipping can and leave for 4 seconds. Then lift out, making sure the wicks do not touch. Leave to cool for 3–4 minutes by balancing the wood across two stands - bottles are ideal.

Step 4

Check the wax is still at 71°C (160°F) and repeat this dipping and cooling process until your candles have reached the desired thickness - usually 1.5–2cm (0.5 – 0.75″) in diameter.

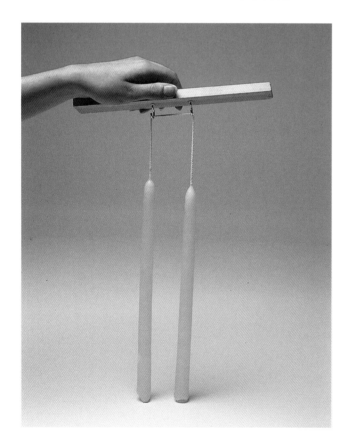

Step 5

To give your candles a shiny finish, heat the wax to 82°C (180°F) for the final two dips. When cool, trim the bases flat and cut wick to 6.5cm ($^{1}/_{4}$″).

You may find the surface becomes lumpy. If this happens, smooth out the bumps while the wax is still warm and then re-dip.

Taper Variations

To create a more unusual candle, tapers can be adapted in several ways.
Here we look at three ideas.

■ ■ ■

Twisted tapers

While your taper is still warm, you can twist it for
an unusual table display.

Step 3

Starting from the top, gently twist the flattened part of the candle. Then trim the base and allow to cool.

If the candle cracks while rolling it is because the wax is too cold. To correct this dip the candle for about 3 seconds at 71°C (160°F) and let it cool for a further half minute.

Step 1

After you have just made your dipped taper candle, let it cool for 30 seconds then place on a sheet of greaseproof paper. Wet your rolling pin.

Step 2

Leaving about 5cm (2″) at the base, gently roll the pin over the rest of the candle, flattening it to about 12cm (1/2″) thickness.

Plaited tapers

If you are feeling adventurous, it is possible to plait three taper candles together.

Step 1

While the candles are still warm, either tie the wicks to a hook, or enlist a friend to hold them for you. Then plait gently.

Step 2

After plaiting, squeeze the bottom ends together to make a base. Three different colours look particularly striking.

Scented tapers

For a delicious, warm aroma, tapers can be coated in cinnamon before burning.
These will enhance any festive occasion.

Step 1

Sprinkle some greaseproof paper with ground cinnamon.

Step 2

Then, while your taper is still warm, simply roll it across the paper. The cinnamon will stick to the warm wax.

Overdipped Candle

Overdipping is a process that involves coating a candle in one or more different colour waxes; usually colours that contrast strongly. By making careful incisions into the dipped wax you can reveal the colour underneath to striking effect.

■　　■　　■

YOU WILL NEED

Dipping can

Large saucepan

Thermometer

Sharp scalpel/craft knife

Double boiler

Orange cylinder candle

Black pigment

Wax beads

Step 1

Make an orange cylinder candle, following steps for a single colour candle as shown.

Step 3

After the fifth dip, let the candle cool for 1 minute. Next, using the scalpel, carefully cut a shape into the warm outer layer that you have just made. Start with something simple like a square.

Step 4

Gently lift out the wax shape you have cut to reveal the colour of the candle below.

Step 2

Put the wax beads and pigment into the dipping can and heat to 78–80°C (172–176°F). The liquid wax inside the can should be deep enough to cover the cylinder candle plus an extra inch or two. Holding by the wick, dip the orange candle into the dipping wax until fully submerged and hold for about 3 seconds. Lift out, let cool for about 20 seconds then repeat the dip four more times. Allow the candle 20 seconds cooling time in between dips.

Step 5

Once you have mastered the technique, try experimenting with different shapes and patterns. When lit, the bright colour of the overdipped candle should seem to glow.

Mushroom
Candles

Mushrooms are fun and easy to make. The trick is to use the wax at just the right temperature before it hardens. One of the most enjoyable elements of this type of candle is the pleasant feeling of the soft wax between your fingers. If you have children and wish to involve them, there are now fun waxes especially designed for them. These waxes are available in different colours, and are warmed in a saucepan. The wax is like warm plasticine and allows children to make their own mushrooms.

■ ■ ■

YOU WILL NEED

Small baking tray(s)
Foil
Sharp knife
Spoon
Wicking needle
Double boiler
Chalky white dye
Red dye disc
Stearin
¹/₂″ wick
Wax beads

Step 1
Line your baking tray with foil. Dissolve the chalky white dye and stearin, then add the wax beads and heat to 82°C (180°F). Prime your wick, cutting it into 10cm (4″) lengths. Pour white wax into a baking tray to a depth of 0.5cm (¹/4″) and let cool until it has a rubbery texture.

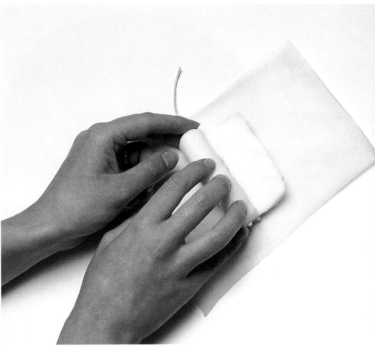

Step 2

Using your knife, cut out a 7.5 x 5cm (3 x 2″) chunk. Gently lift this out and place on greaseproof paper.

Step 3

Place wick along the short side and roll the wax around tightly, making sure half the wick protrudes from one side. Stand on end and level the base. This will be your stalk.

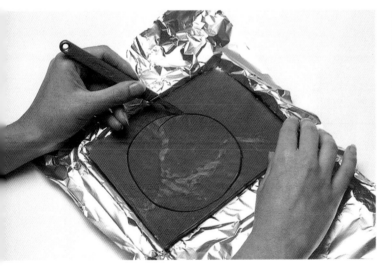

Step 4

Dissolve the red dye and stearin and heat wax to 80°C (176°F). Pour into foil lined baking tray to a depth of 0.5cm ($^1/4$″), and let cool until rubbery. Cut a 7.5cm (3″) circle in the wax and place on greaseproof paper.

Step 5

Gently mould the red cap into the shape of a mushroom top and let cool.

Step 6

Make a hole through the centre of the red cap, and thread through the exposed wick of the stalk. To bind the stalk to the cap, turn upside down and hold the two parts together firmly. Spoon some of the left-over warm wax into the underside of the cap and allow to cool.

Step 7

When your binding wax has cooled, trim your wick as normal.

Variations

To give your mushroom stalk a smoother appearance, try overdipping it in clear wax a few times before fastening the mushroom cap. To decorate the cap with spots, either use white acrylic poster paint, or drip small dots of white wax onto the cap, and allow to cool.

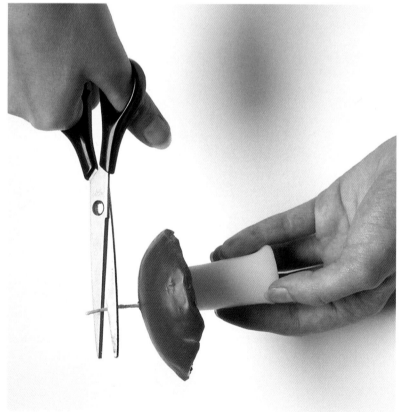

Peeled Banana Candle

Making a peeled banana combines many of the techniques we have been practising to produce an amusing and decorative candle.

■ ■ ■

YOU WILL NEED

(to make 4 bananas):
Double boiler
2 dipping cans
Rubber banana mould
Cardboard support
Scalpel/craft knife
Bowl of water
Thermometer
Wicking needle
2 large saucepans
5kg (12.5lb) dip and carve wax
350g (12oz) paraffin wax beads
Half cream dye disc
1 and a half chalky white dye discs
1 yellow dye disc
Vybar
1″ wick

Step 1

Wick up the mould and put it into the cardboard support. Melt the paraffin wax beads and vybar in the double boiler. Add 1g (0.04 oz) of the cream dye disc and 2.5g (0.1 oz) of the chalky white dye disc and heat to 90°C (194°F). Pour into the mould, tap out air bubbles, and place in water bath, with support across. Leave to cool, breaking the surface and topping up as necessary. When the wax fruit is cold, rub

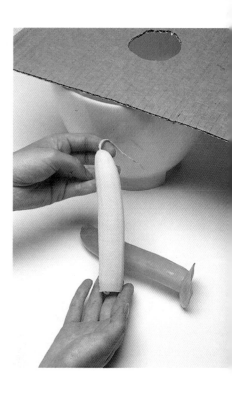

some washing up liquid onto the outside of the mould and peel the mould away.

Step 2

For the skin we will use both dipping cans at the same time. In one place 2.5kg (6lb 4oz) of dip and carve wax; 18g (0.8 oz) of the chalky white dye disc and 5g (0.2 oz) of the yellow dye disc. This will be the inner layer of the skin. In the second dipping can place 2.5kg (6lb 4 oz) of dip and carve wax, 7.5g (0.3 oz) of the yellow dye disc, 3.7g (0.13 oz) of the chalky white dye disc and 7g (0.3 oz) of the cream dye disc. Put the dipping cans in the saucepans. Half fill the saucepans with water and heat the wax to 67°C (153°F). Maintain this temperature throughout the dipping.

Step 3

Dip your banana fruit into cold water. Then, holding by the wick, dip in and out of the first inner layer dipping can. Let cool for between 45 seconds to 1 minute, then repeat this process another six times.

Step 4

After the last dip in the inner layer wax, leave to cool for a minute. Then dip into the outside layer dipping can. Repeat this 8–10 times, leaving 1 minute between dips. After the last dip let the candle cool for about 5–8 minutes.

Step 5

Starting from the top of the banana, gently cut through the warm skin to about three quarters of the way down. Repeat this twice more around the banana.

Step 6

Again starting from the top, peel back the first strip of the banana skin, curling as you go. Repeat for the second strip..

Step 7

Repeat step 6 for the second strip. Once you have peeled and curled the third strip, allow to cool for several minutes. Your candle is now complete.

CHAPTER SIX

Special Effects *and* Techniques

■ ■ ■

INTRODUCTION

There are many different techniques for producing stunning effects and finishes on candles. Some involve using special waxes, readily available from craft shops, which are simply applied to a fininshed candle, either by hand, or by dipping.

We will look at different ways of decorating candles, both with paints, stickers and more unusual materials such as sand and shells, together with ways of creating unique candle patterns and shapes without the use of conventional moulds.

Some of these techniques will require practice to perfect, so it is a good idea to practice first on old or damaged candles. As you work on these projects you will begin to master the effects, so can go on to experiment with your own ideas and designs. As several of these projects involve using melted wax in different ways to those

you have become familiar with, you will need to take special care to avoid spillages and burns.

Decorative effects for unusual finishes

Dipping with Special Waxes

There are now on the market waxes that can be used to create interesting effects on the surface of candles when dipped. This overdipping method is ideal for livening up plain candles, or giving a new finish to candles that have been marked or pitted. In this project we will use a commercial wax, called Snowflake wax. This can be coloured like ordinary wax. Special waxes are generally rather expensive, but you can achieve similar effects by using materials you are already familiar with.

■   ■   ■

YOU WILL NEED

Equipment as for standard dipping

Snowflake wax

Step 1

Heat up the wax in your dipping can to 67°C (153°F). Take a coloured candle and dip it in and out once.

Step 2

Place to one side and leave. You will see that the special wax has dries into a snowflake pattern.

Try experimenting with the temperature. By increasing the heat, the snowflake pattern will be more intense. A slightly lower temperature will create larger snowflakes.

Variations

If you are feeling more artistic, you can run streaks of contrasting colour wax down the surface of your candle.

If you do not wish to use special waxes, heat concentrated stearin in a dipping can to 77–80°C (172–176°F) and dip a strong coloured candle in and out. Leave to cool as above. As the waxcools you will get a tough, crystalline effect.

Using Gilding Wax

Gilding wax is available in tubes, and is easy to apply with your fingertip. It is especially effective on dark coloured candles, and by using a variety of household objects you can create any number of patterns, from simple line scoring, to complex swirls. We have chosen a fork to create our pattern, but try experimenting with a wire brush, a screw, a comb or even sandpaper.

■ ■ ■

YOU WILL NEED

Fork

Fine paint brush

Plain black candle

Gilding wax

Step 1

Take the fork and etch lines in the candle with a downward stroke. Turn the fork gently as you score, to create wavy lines.

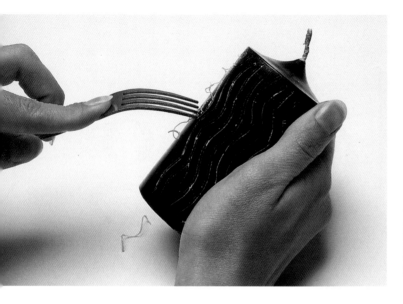

Step 2
Work your way around the candle, keeping the lines as evenly spaced as possible.

Step 3
After you have created your pattern, use the fine paint brush to brush away the wax residue before you start gilding.

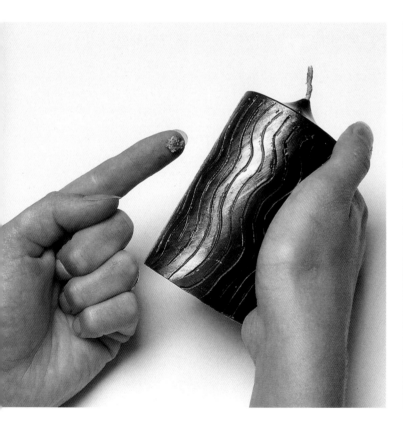

Step 4
Squeeze some gilt onto your finger, and lightly work into the surface of the candle. You will see the pattern begin to emerge.

Step 5
If you want a deeper effect, cover very lightly with a second coat. You can also use gilding wax on any candle with a pattern in relief.

Quick *and* Easy Gilt Effects

Another way of obtaining a metallic decorative finish is to use wax stickers. These are available on strips of specially treated paper, and are quick and simple to use.

Step 1
Warm your wax stickers to room temperature. This will make them flexible, and should prevent them from snapping or breaking.

Step 2
Peel each sticker off carefully, avoiding stretching or breaking your shape.

Step 3
Press gently but firmly in place on your candle. Use as few or as many stickers as you wish, to produce a unique effect.

Ice
Candles

You can achieve stunning random effects with ice. Where the hot wax meets the ice, it cools and hardens rapidly. When the ice has melted, the wax is full of cavities that create interesting and unique patterns in your candle.

■   ■   ■

YOU WILL NEED

Plastic bag or towel

Hammer

Double boiler

Ice cubes

Wax beads

Stearin

Cylindrical mould

Dye disc

Mould seal

Blue $^1/_2''$ wick

Step 1

Dissolve the dye and stearin in the double boiler. Add the wax beads and heat to 93°C (199°F). Prime your wick, then wick up and seal your mould.

Step 2

Place the ice in a plastic bag, or wrap in the towel and smash it with a hammer.

Step 3

Place the ice loosely into the mould.

Step 4

Pour the melted wax into the mould and wait until the wax is cold and the ice has melted.

Step 5

Gently slide out of mould.
Trim wick and put aside to
dry before burning.

Pour in Pour out

Here we will be adapting the basic method of making a candle in a rubber mould to create a colourful and unusual effect. For this you will need to use two different colours. Experiment with colours to produce a variety of effects, ranging from the pastel coolness of the colours selected for this project, to a more dramatic finish.

■   ■   ■

YOU WILL NEED

**Bowl of water, deep enough to
hold your mould**

Cardboard support

2 double boilers

Scissors

Wicking needle

Rubber mould

Chalky white dye disc

Violet dye disk

Vybar

Wax beads

Wick

Washing up liquid and water mix

Step I

If you have not already done so, make a cardboard support for your mould. Using your wicking needle, wick up the mould and fit into the cardboard support.

Step 2

Heat up both double boilers, melting the violet dye, vybar and wax beads in one, and the chalky white dye, vybar and wax beads in the other, both to a temperature of 85°C (185°F). Remove from the heat and pour the white wax into your mould, placing it in the water bath. It will not take long for the outside layer to start solidifying.

Step 3

When the outside wax has set to a depth of about 5mm (0.2″), remove the mould with support from the water and pour out the liquid wax.

Step 4

Refill the mould with the violet wax and place in the water bath to set, remembering to break the surface and top up when necessary.

Step 5

When cool, rub washing up liquid mix on the outside of the mould and peel back the mould. Even off your base.

Stencilling Candles

To turn even the simplest candle into something special, you can stencil a pattern onto any plain candle with a smooth surface. Acrylic poster paints are ideal, or you can use the gilding paste from a previous project. Stencils are available from craft shops, DIY stores, or alternatively you can make your own.

■ ■ ■

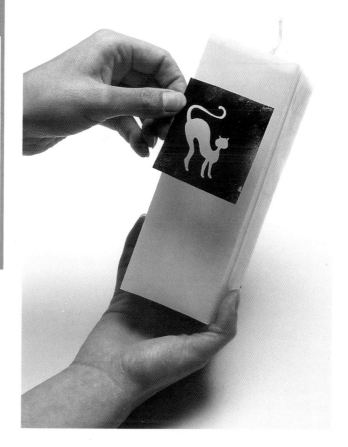

YOU WILL NEED

Stencils

Cloth

Paint brush

White candle (any size)

Coloured paint

Step 1

Choose your stencil design and where you are going to place it on the candle.

Step 2

Select a colour from your paints and paint over the stencil. It is a good idea to work from the edges to the middle of the stencil to avoid paint creeping underneath.

Step 3

Remove the stencil, being careful not to smudge your design.

Variations

Once you have mastered this technique using commercial stencils, try creating your own to complement themes or patterns in your home.

Shell Candles

As we have seen, a wax surface lends itself to all kinds of decoration. Most people have pleasant memories of collecting shells from the beach, and a shell candle makes an excellent momento of an enjoyable trip or holiday.

■ ■ ■

YOU WILL NEED

Large saucepan

Thermometer

Scalpel

Marker pen

Wax beads

Blue cylinder candle

Small shells (cleaned and dried)

Step 1
With the marker pen, dot the candle where you wish to place your shells.

Step 2

When you are satisfied with your design, take the scalpel and gouge small holes in the surface.

Step 3

Place one of your shells over a previously marked hole, and outline around it with the scalpel. Gouge out enough wax to make a hole deep and wide enough for it to stay in place, but still be proud of the surface. Push into place.

Step 4

Repeat step 2 until all your shells are in place.

Variations

A shell can also make a pretty display candle. Cut a piece of wick long enough to reach the bottom of the shell and suspend centrally over the shell with a wicking needle. Fill with plain or coloured wax, adding scent if you wish.

Making a
Realistic
Snail

Wax is an excellent medium for painting. Paint can either be used to highlight details or for putting the finishing touches to realistic models - animals for example. This project utilises both methods. Animal moulds and many others are readily available from craft shops.

■ ■ ■

YOU WILL NEED

Snail candle mould

Scalpel

Paint brush (reasonably wide)

Old towel or cloth

Acrylic paints – dark brown, light brown and green

Black poster paint

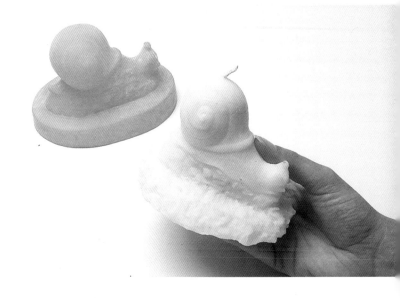

Step 1

Make the snail in the mould using white wax, following instructions from previous rubber mould projects. Carefully trim excess wax from the base.

Step 2

Paint the whole snail black and allow to dry. Wash brush thoroughly.

Step 3

Rub gently with a towel or cloth. As you rub you will see that while most of the black paint will be removed, the colour will remain in the detailed parts of the candle.

Step 4

Take the acrylic paints and first paint the shell light brown, then the body dark brown. Wash brush. Then paint the grass dark green.

Step 5

You may wish to finish off your candle with a candle glaze. This is available from craft shops and is a kind of varnish that both imparts a gloss finish to your candle, and helps to protect it.

Hammering Candles

You will probably have noticed that when you drop candles or knock them by accident, they whiten at the point of impact. Believe it or not, this unfortunate accident can be made into a deliberately striking effect. Before trying this technique on a good candle, experiment a few time using a couple of old candles you no longer need.

■ ■ ■

YOU WILL NEED

Ball point hammer

Second hammer

A plain candle

Step 1

Place the ball of the hammer on the candle, then tap lightly but firmly with the other hammer. Use enough force to cause a round white indented circle to appear on the candle surface at the point of impact. Using two hammers helps to achieve accuracy in your design.

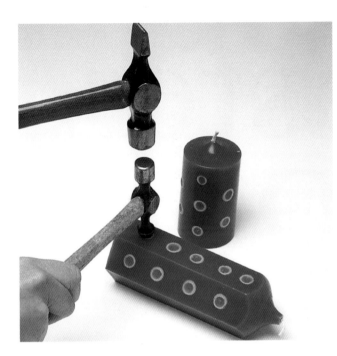

Step 2

When you combine lots of these indentations either randomly or in lines, you get a striking effect on your candle with the white offset against the dark background.

Tips

Use a flat sided candle to begin with rather than a cone or cylinder, as this will make balancing the candle much easier.

Use a candle that has been warmed to room temperature, as this effect is harder to achieve on a cold candle.

Easter Eggs

Come Easter time, the techniques you have learnt for making and decorating candles can be put together make a special Easter display. This project is one that children will particularly enjoy helping with!

■　■　■

YOU WILL NEED

Plastic egg moulds

Half inch wick

Various dye disks

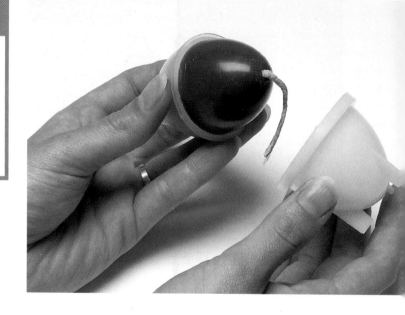

Step 1

With the egg moulds, make up a selection of egg candles using the methods from previous projects.

Step 2

Decorate using the methods described in earlier projects – dipping, gilding and painting.

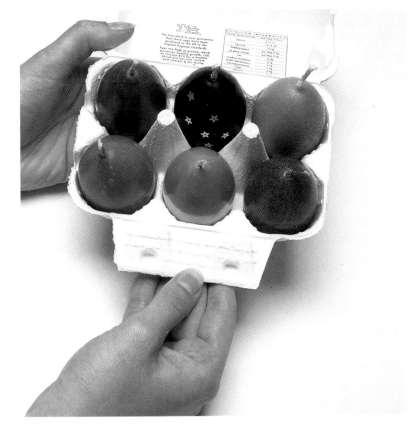

Step 3

An egg box makes for an amusing display of your candles, as do baskets or eggcups.

Water Candles

With practice, you can create spectacular feathery clouds or sculptures of delicate wax plumes by making water candles. As you plunge the hot wax into the water it is drawn to the surface where it cools rapidly into random patterns. The results are unpredictable but always dramatic. When pouring the hot wax, it may be a good idea to wear rubber gloves to avoid burning your fingers.

■   ■   ■

YOU WILL NEED

Deep bucket of water

Double boiler

Bowl

Foil

Thermometer

Towel

Wax beads

Chalky white dye disc

Taper candle

Stearin

Rubber gloves

Step 1

Line your bowl with foil.

Step 2

Dissolve the white dye and stearin. Add wax beads and heat to 80°C (176°F). Fix your taper candle into the centre of the bowl by using a little of the liquid wax.

Step 3

Once the candle is secure, fill the bowl with 5cm (2″) of liquid wax.

Step 4

Plunge the bowl into the bucket of water. For a variation, twist the bowl as you plunge it – but always keep the bowl upright.

Step 5

Bring the bowl out of the bucket and gently drain off some water. Leave to cool. Ease the foil out of the bowl. Remove from wax and let candle dry on a towel.

Variation

For an interesting "wrap" effect, try pouring melted wax directly onto your taper candle.

Step 1

Place a taper in a bowl of water wide enough that the candle does not touch the sides.

Step 2

Then gently pour the wax onto the candle, starting at the middle, and avoiding your fingers! Twist the candle as you pour, and gradually work down to the base of the candle. As the wax hits the water, it cools into flexible strands that wrap around the taper.

Sand Candles

The striking appearance of a sand candle is especially satisfying as the method used is easy and fun. Quite simply, a shape is hollowed into damp sand, and molten wax is poured into this hole. As the wax cools, the sand around the wax is stuck to the surface, creating an unusual patterned finish.

■ ■ ■

YOU WILL NEED

Bowl half filled with sand

Double boiler

Thermometer

Piece of wood/cane slightly larger than the diameter of the bowl

Tape measure

Wax beads

Dye disc

Vybar

2″ wick (primed)

Water

Step 1

Dampen the sand in your bowl with water, then carefully form a rounded hole in the sand. Make sure the bottom of the bowl is not exposed. Pat the sides flat firmly.

Step 2

For added balance, candles can be made with legs. Leave about 12.5cm (5 ″) of sand beneath your formed bowl, and with a thin candle or a reasonably thick piece of wood make three or four holes under the bowl. Again, ensure that the bottom of the bowl is not exposed. These holes will fill with wax, and form the legs when the candle is removed.

Step 3

Place the cane across the top of the bowl and measure from the bottom of the sand shape to the cane. This will be your wick height. Leaving enough wick for tying the cane, cut the wick. Tie one end to the cane, making sure that the wick touches the bottom of the sand shape, and lies central within it.

Step 4

Heat the wax beads, dye and vybar in the double boiler to 100°C (212°F), then pour into the sand, being careful not to disturb the sides or the wick. Leave for 5 minutes. During this time some of the wax will have seeped into the sand. Top up to the original level, then leave to cool. When the well appears in the candle, heat up your wax to 93°C (199°F) and top up once more.

Step 5

When the candle is cool, remove from the sand, gently brush off excess sand and level off.

Variations

Try using coloured sand, or even gravel for different effects.

Foil Candles

Foil can be used to create unusual shapes that can be used as table decorations, or even as floating candles.

■ ■ ■

YOU WILL NEED

Bowl half filled with sand

Double boiler

Thermometer

Piece of wood/cane slightly larger
than the diameter of the bowl

Tape measure

Wax beads

Dye disc

Vybar

Water

1/2" wick

Tin foil

Step 1

Dampen the sand and make round wells of about 5cm (2″) deep by 5cm (2″) wide. Line these wells with a piece of tin foil.

Step 2

Place your wick over each well, one end touching the base, the other tied to the wicking needle. Heat up your wax, stearin and dye to 82°C (180°F). Being careful not to disturb your wick, pour in the wax and leave to cool.

Step 3

When cooled, remove from the sand and peel off the tin foil.

Variations

Try experimenting with different colours and sizes to create an eye-catching display!

Moulds around the House

You do not have to purchase special moulds to create attractive candles. A look around the house or garden will reveal a number of everyday objects which can be just as effective. Here we have chosen a simple terracotta flower pot.

■ ■ ■

YOU WILL NEED

Double boiler

Thermometer

Small 3" flower pot

Wax beads

Dye discs

Vybar

1" wick

Candle scent/paints (optional)

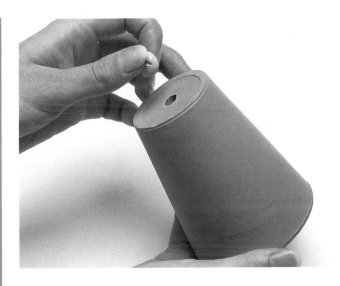

Step 1
Most pots have a hole in the bottom. This must be plugged with putty before you begin.

Step 2

Fill the flower pot with wax, as for previous projects using moulds. Add the scent if required.

Variations

Flowerpots are not the only household objects that make ideal candle moulds. However, there are some important guidelines to remember. Most importantly, be sure that whatever you use is able to withstand the temperature of the hot wax. Your mould should have no holes for wax

Step 3

For decoration, apply acrylic paints with a fine, flat brush to create a lively pattern on your pot, and for an extra effect, try wrapping rough twine around the top.

to leak from, and should be wider or as wide at the top as it is at the bottom otherwise your candle will not come out. As a rule, if your intended mould can withstand boiling hot water, then it is suitable for wax.

An empty juice carton makes an ideal mould, as the carton can be simply torn away when the candle has cooled.

Old yoghurt or cream tubs can also be used. It may be useful to use two wicks if using a wide tub or pot. This will make the candle easier to remove, and will create an interesting effect when lit.

CHAPTER SEVEN

Working *with* Beeswax

Beeswax has been used for centuries in the art of candle making, and has had both a cultural and religious significance. A natural product, available in shades of either brown or bleached white, it has a pleasing smell, and is long-burning with a smokeless flame.

■ ■ ■

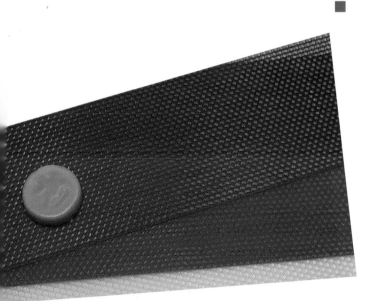

Beeswax comes in either sheets or blocks

Today, as throughout its history, it is an expensive material. In the Middle Ages only the rich could afford beeswax candles, as there were no moulds and they had to be crafted by hand. Indeed, such was their value, they could even be used by candle-makers in lieu of their tithe payment to the church. Nowadays modern church candles contain only around 25% beeswax, as it is combined with other waxes to increase burning time.

Beeswax comes in two forms – either blocks or sheets, each available in a variety of different colours. Beeswax sheets form the basis of our next projects, as they are the most enjoyable form to work with. Not only do they smell and look wonderful, they are tactile and easily decorated to produce stunning and imaginative candles.

Instead of dirt and poison we have rather chosen to fill our hives with honey and wax; thus furnishing mankind with the two noblest of things, which are sweetness and light.

Jonathan Swift, The Draper's Letters

Rolled Beeswax Candle

Step 1

Warm your beeswax sheet near a radiator or fire, or heat with a hairdryer on a low setting. This will make it more supple and therefore easier to work with. Beeswax warms very quickly and a few minutes' gentle heating should suffice.

Step 2

Place the sheet on a clean, hard and flat surface such as a coffee table. Then place the wick along the edge of the beeswax, leaving the extra wick length protruding.

Step 3

Roll the beeswax tightly around the wick to the end of the sheet.

Step 4

To finish, use your fingertips to stick the edge of the sheet to the main candle body. The texture of the beeswax sheet gives it excellent adhesion.

Tapered Beeswax Candle

This makes an attractive variation on the previous project.

■ ■ ■

YOU WILL NEED

Sharp knife

Ruler

Beeswax sheet

Primed wick as Project 1

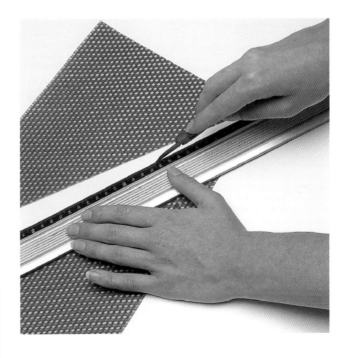

Step 1

Using the ruler as a guide, cut your beeswax sheet diagonally.

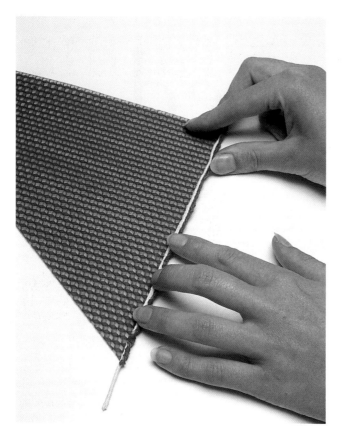

Step 2

Place the wick along the shortest edge of the beeswax sheet, leaving about 2.5cm (1″) protruding.

Step 3

Roll the beeswax firmly around the wick, making sure to keep the bottom of the candle even.

Step 4

Secure the end by pushing the end flap of the beeswax sheet firmly into the main candle.

Decorating Beeswax Candles

The previous two projects show just two kinds of beeswax candles you can make very quickly and easily. By cutting your beeswax sheet, or rolling several sheets together, you can create any size of candle you wish.

■ ■ ■

While beeswax candles themselves are attractive, there are also many ways to decorate them. By experimenting with different colours, materials and sizes, you can create beautiful displays for your own home, or charming and original gifts for friends.

There is no limit – except your imagination – to how many ways a candle can be decorated, although here we suggest a few tried and tested favourites:

1) Raffia/Dried Lavender
2) Ribbon/leaves
3) Cloves
4) Contrasting colour beeswax strips

The best way to secure objects to your candle is either by tying with twine or ribbon, or fastening with small pins.

REMEMBER – ALWAYS REMOVE FLAMMABLE MATERIALS BEFORE CANDLES IS LIT

CHAPTER EIGHT

Advanced Procedures

After working through the projects in this book, you should by now have become reasonably proficient in the basic candle making methods, techniques and materials, and you may wish to proceed further.

■ ■ ■

Many people will be satisfied with experimenting with the techniques shown in this book, and adapting them to create unique designs of their own. However, some of you may choose to pursue candle-making to a more advanced stage, so we will briefly look at some extra equipment available to you.

This equipment will not only save time, but will help you make better candles and enable you to achieve some professional finishes.

You have already seen that moulds can be produced from ordinary household objects such and juice cartons or flowerpots. The next step you will probably wish to take is that of making your own moulds. The next project explains clearly how to do this.

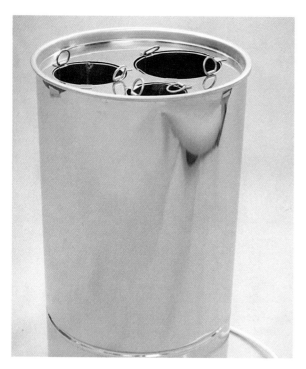

Dipping Station

You will know from your experiences with overdipping that before changing colour you have to remove the old pigment and start again. However, there is on the market a piece of equipment called a dipping station. This is basically a large kettle, usually holding four dipping cans. It has a heating control that you fill with water, and this heats the wax in the cans to the desired temperature. This is very useful for overdipping several colours at the same time.

Pouring Jugs

Another extremely useful item to buy is a pouring jug. These jugs are available in various liquid capacities, and normally have a spout which helps eliminate wax spillage when pouring into moulds.

Wax Boiler

If you are making lots of candles, you might look at buying a wax boiler, although these are expensive. They hold up to 100kg of wax, have a thermostat and are water heated. Wax exits from a large tap.

Making Your Own Moulds

At some stage you are probably going to want to make your own moulds. Maybe you will have an object that you think would be an interesting shape for a candle, or you will have made something yourself especially for this purpose. The easiest material to use for a mould is liquid latex, which is available in various quantities. This will give you a rubber skin mould.

■　■　■

YOU WILL NEED

Paint brush

Liquid latex

Plasticine/double-sided sticky tape

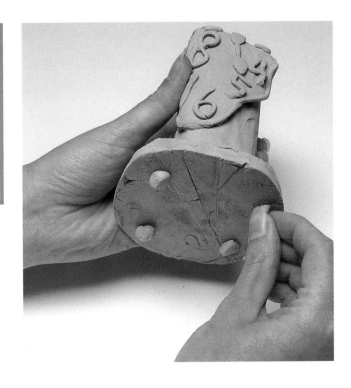

Step 1

Secure your object down on a smooth surface with plasticine or double-sided sticky tape.

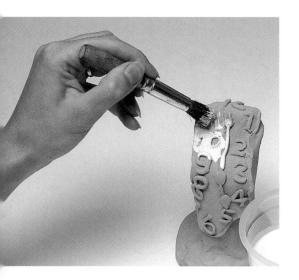

Step 2

Take the paintbrush and dip into the liquid latex. Working thoroughly into any crevices, cover your model and two inches around the base and leave to dry. Wash brush immediately.

Step 3

Liquid latex is air drying. The thinner the coat the quicker it will dry. Repeat this process until the mould is approximately 2mm thick.

Step 4

Peel off mould using washing up liquid. Clean and dry, and allow to cure at room temperature for at least 72 hours.

Things to watch out for:

If your model has deep undercuts, or holes, you cannot make a mould
as you will be unable to remove it

If your model is too big your mould will distort once wax is poured into it

Do not touch the rubber between coats as this will affect adhesion

Taking moulds from metal may cause problems as chemicals in the latex may react

Untreated/unpainted plaster models give the best results

Skin moulds will not last as long as commercial moulds

CHAPTER NINE

Problems *and* How *to* Solve Them

MOULD TIPS AND PROBLEMS

If you are having trouble removing the candle from the mould, try placing it in the freezer for 10-15 minutes. This should shrink the wax so that a gentle tap will release the candle.

Though quite expensive, a silicon spray or similar releasing agent applied to the mould before pouring will aid release, and keep moulds clean.

Always keep your moulds clean, but be careful not to scratch them as the marks will show on every subsequent candle.

Metal moulds can be cleaned by placing in a hot oven for a few minutes and then wiping them round with a kitchen towel. With soldered metal moulds, be careful that you do not melt the solder!

If you use rubber moulds a lot you will notice that they stretch, making your candles larger. Though a cold water bath retards this stretching a little, you cannot stop it completely. The heat causes them to stretch and eventually rot.

Be careful when wicking up and de-moulding rubber moulds not to make a hole in the rubber.

Always use a lubricating agent such as washing up liquid to aid release.

Make sure there are no kinks in your rubber mould and that it is fully pushed out, or the heat from the wax will cause your mould to tear.

COMMON CANDLE PROBLEMS

Wax has leaked around the base

Pitted surface

There is a thin layer of wax dripped around the candle base.
The candle was topped up above the original wax level, and wax has leaked down between the candle and the mould after contraction. Cut off the drips and buff with a nylon stocking.

My candle has a pitted surface.
The wax was probably too cold when poured.

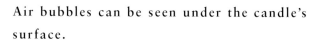

Air bubbles

White lines between colours

Air bubbles can be seen under the candle's surface.
It was not tapped enough before being placed in the water bath. Alternatively the wax was poured too fast.

On a multi coloured candle, there are white lines where the different colour waxes meet.
The second wax was poured in at too low a temperature

When heating the wax it hisses or bubbles.
There are impurities or water in the wax.
Throw wax away, or use it for chunks.
Check wax source.

Scum or froth appears on the surface.
As before, except remove scum with spoon.

I have wax leaking from my mould.
Check mould seal.

There is a fine line around the candle.
The water level of the bath could have been lower than the level of the wax in the mould.

Surface becomes lumpy while dipping
Either the wax was too cold or the first dip was too fast. Smooth out bumps while the wax is still warm and then re-dip.

The candle will not come out of the mould.
First make sure the mould seal has been removed. If so, it may be that not enough stearin was added to the wax. Try putting the candle into the fridge for 20 minutes. Alternatively place in hot water until the candle slides out.

The rubber mould will not come off.
Try using more washing up liquid. It may be that your mould has been damaged or has begun to rot. Check inside the mould for whiteness or holes.

The candle won't light.
Check the wick for mould seal and clean. Check that the wick has been primed. If not, hold the candle upside down and then light.

The candle flame is too large.
Possible the wick used is too large for the candle, or the wick needs to be trimmed back down to a quarter of an inch.

Candle cracks

There are cracks in the candle.
The candle became too cold before topping up.

The candle flame is very small.
Either the wick is too small, or impurities in the candle have clogged the wick. Use larger wick.

The candle burns unevenly.
Check for draughts, and that the wick is positioned centrally.

The candle spits while burning.
This is most likely to happen with ice or water candles. It probably means there is water in the wax. Extinguish the candle and tip out the molten wax. Re-light. If the spitting continues, throw candle away.

Avoid impurities or water in your wax

An even flame is easy to achieve

Remember that if melting different colour waxes, the resulting colour will almost always be brown.

Don't allow candle to become too cold before topping up

WARNING
· · · · · · · · ·

NEVER LEAVE CANDLES UNATTENDED

∎

PLACE CANDLES ON A SECURE BASE AWAY FROM
THE REACH OF CHILDREN, PETS AND DRAUGHTS

∎

ORNAMENTAL CANDLES MAY BURN ERRATICALLY

∎

REMOVE ALL FLAMMABLE MATERIALS FROM
CANDLES BEFORE LIGHTING

∎

IF IN DOUBT – EXTINGUISH

Glossary

■ ■ ■

Beeswax – natural wax product.

De-moulding – removing finished candle from mould.

Dipping can – tall, cylindrical, metal vessel for holding hot wax.

Dipping station – electrically heated container, holding several dipping cans. Used when overdipping several colours at the same time.

Double Boiler – double saucepan set for melting wax over heat source.

Dye disk – solid mix of colour and stearin used for tinting candle wax.

Gilding wax – special wax, available in tubes that can be applied with the fingers to produce dramatic effects.

Heat Source – for melting paraffin wax. A domestic cooker is ideal.

Latex – in liquid form, available in various quantities and ideal for creating your own moulds.

Mould seal – putty-like substance used to hold wick in place and prevent wax seeping from moulds.

Moulds – shaped holders for molten wax. Commercial moulds come in a range of materials, shapes and sizes.

Overdipping – process of coating a candles with a contrasting coloured wax.

Overdipping wax – combination of resins and waxes that produce a tough and shiny coating.

Paraffin wax – by-product of crude petroleum.

Pigment – used to colour overdipping wax. Stronger than dye, and produces a more intense colour.

Pour in-pour out – process of combining coloured waxes by allowing the outer layer of the first batch of wax to cool, then pouring out the remaining liquid wax. A second colour is then added.

Pouring jugs – specialist jugs of varying capacities, particularly useful when using

Use overdipping wax to create elegant taper candles

larger quantities of hot wax.

Priming – process of preparing a wick for usage.

Scent-and-dye disks – dye disks that contain an aromatic oil - eliminates need for additional scents, and excellent for giving fruit candles an extra finish.

Silicon spray – used as releasing agent to ease removal of candles from glass and metal moulds.

Snowflake overdipping wax – special wax so-called because the finished candle will show a pattern similar to flakes of snow.

Special waxes – commercially available waxes that produce unusual effects on finished candles.

Stearin – Makes wax contract, aiding release from rigid mould. Also used to enhance depth of colour, decrease dripping and improve burning. Not suitable for rubber moulds.

Tallow – substance similar to suet, used in early candles.

Taper – name given to candle produced by dipping.

Thermometer – a specialist wax thermometer is essential.

Vybar – additive used to stop wax contracting, increase wax opacity, and improve burning. Not suitable for rigid moulds.

Wax boiler – electrically heated boilers with a capacity of 100kg of wax. Ideal if candle-making in large batches.

Wick – varied widths and lengths of chemically treated braided cotton.

Wick holder – commercially available to hold wick in place over mould.

Wicking needle – used for inserting wicks into moulds.

Paraffin beads are the easiest form of this wax to use

125

Index

■ ■ ■

A

Air bubbles, 120
Asparagus boiler, 14

B

Beeswax, 6, 8, 14
  Decorating, 111
  Rolled candle, 107-108
  Tapered candle, 109-110
  Working with, 105-106

C

Cambaceres, 7
Candere, 6
Candles,
  Angled multi-coloured, 29-31
  Bead, 36-38
  Burning of, 12, 122
  Chunk & Dye, 34-35
  Church, 44-46
  Cracks in, 121
  Dipped, 49
  Easter Eggs, 90-91
  Floating, 41-43
  Foil, 100-102
  Fruit, 47-48
  Hammering, 88-89
  Ice, 73-75
  Multi-coloured, 26-28, 120
  Mushroom, 58-61

Overdipped, 55-57
Peeled banana, 62-64
Pour-in,Pour-out, 76-78
Problems with, 118-122
Sand, 96-99
Scented, 39-40
Shell, 82-84
Single colour cone, 23-25
Snail realistic, 85-87
Stencilling, 79-81
Water, 92-95

D

Dipping can, 14

Dipping station, 114

Double boiler, 13

Dye discs, 18, 49

E

Effects, special, 65

J

Jug,

Measuring, 15

Pouring, 114

L

Lines, white, 120, 121

M

Morgan, Joseph, 7

Mouldseal, 18, 121

Moulds, 14

Around the house, 103-104

Glass, 18

Latex, 18, 115-117

Metal, 18, 118

Plastic, 18

Problems, 118

Rubber, 18, 118, 119, 121

O

Overdipping, 49, 51, 67

P

Pigment, 49

S

Scales, 14

Scalpel, 15

Shakespeare, 9

Silicon spray, 118

Stearin, 18

T

Tallow, 6, 17

Tapers, 49

Dipped dinner, 50-52

Variations, 53-54

Thermometer, 11, 13

Turpentine, 11

V

Vybar, 18

W

Wax,

Boiler, 114

Gilding, 69-71

Heating of, 1, 13, 120

Leaking of, 119, 121

Overdipping, 49

Removal of, 11

Snowflake, 67

Special, 65, 66-69

Spillage of, 10, 11

Stickers, gilt, 72

Temperature of, 120, 121

White spirit, 11

Wick, 18

Braided, 7

Priming, 21

Wicking needle, 14

Credits and Acknowledgements

The authors would like to thank the following for
supplying the materials used in these projects:

E.H. Thorne (Beehives) Ltd
Lincolnshire
(Beeswax and general candle making equipment)

Rodwins
London
(General candle and craft supplies)

Hayes and Finch
Liverpool
(Wicks)

Dussek Campbell Ltd
Lancashire
(Wax manufacturers)

The Banana Candle Firm
London
(Bananas and fruit candles)